J
591
.1078
W

Wood, Robert W.

Science for kids : 39 easy animal
    biology experiments

39 EASY
ANIMAL BIOLOGY EXPERIMENTS

Science for Kids
39 EASY
ANIMAL BIOLOGY
EXPERIMENTS

Robert W. Wood
Illustrated by Steve Hoeft

TAB BOOKS
Blue Ridge Summit, PA

FIRST EDITION
FIRST PRINTING

Library of Congress Cataloging-in-Publication Data

Wood, Robert W. 1933-
    Science for kids : 39 easy animal biology experiments / by Robert
W. Wood.
        p.   cm.
    Includes index.
    Summary: Step-by-step instructions teach readers how to do
projects that explain the ways animal and human bodies live and
work.
    ISBN 0-8306-6594-3 (h)   ISBN 0-8306-3594-7 (p)
    1. Physiology—Experiments—Juvenile literature.   2. Biology-
-Experiments—Juvenile literature.   3. Animals—Physiology—Juvenile
literature. [1. Physiology—Experiments.   2. Biology—Experiments.
3. Animals—Physiology—Experiments.   4. Experiments.] I. Title.
QP42.W66   1991
591.1′078—dc20   91-11223
                                                             CIP
                                                             AC

TAB Books offers software for sale. For information and a catalog, please contact TAB Software Department, Blue Ridge Summit, PA 17294-0850.

Questions regarding the content of this book should be addressed to:

Acquisitions Editor: Kimberly Tabor
Book Editor: Susan L. Rockwell
Production: Katherine G. Brown
Book Design: Jaclyn J. Boone
Cover photograph by Susan Riley, Harrisonburg, VA.

Contents

Disclaimer

Ethical science practices involve very careful consideration of living organisms. One cannot recklessly cause pain, damage, or death to any living organism.

Adult supervision is advised when working with these projects. No responsibility is implied or taken for anyone who sustains injuries as a result of using the materials or ideas put forward in this book. Taste nothing. Use proper equipment (gloves, safety glasses, and other safety precautions). Clean up broken glass with a dust pan and brush. Use chemicals with extra care. Wash hands after project work is done. Tie up loose hair and clothing. Follow step-by-step procedures; avoid short cuts. Never work alone. Remember, adult supervision is advised. Safety precautions are addressed in the text. If you use common sense and make safety the first consideration, you will create safe, fun, educational, and rewarding projects.

Introduction

The Science For Kids series will consist of eight books introducing Astronomy, Chemistry, Meteorology, Geology, Engineering, Plant Biology, Animal Biology, and Geography.

Science is a subject that instantly becomes exciting with even simple discoveries. On any day, and at any time, we can see these mysteries unfold around us.

The series was written to open the door, and to invite the curious to enter—to explore, to think, and to wonder. To realize that anyone, absolutely anyone at all, can experiment and learn. To discover that the only thing you really need to study science is an inquiring mind. The rest of the material is all around you. It is there for anyone to see. You have to only look.

Biology is the study of living things. The origin, physical characteristics, habits, and life process of plants and animals. It is one of the oldest of the sciences. Even our earliest ancestors were interested in the wonders of plants and animals. Life is one of the great mysteries of the universe. Living things take in food and are nourished. They grow and reproduce their own kind. But they are made up of the same basic chemical elements as nonliving things. When the composition of plants and animals are analyzed by chemists, they find elements commonly found in the earth, sea water, and in the air. These elements usually come together to form compounds. Water, for example, is a compound of hydrogen and oxygen, and makes up between 65 and 90 percent of the weight of most plants and animals. Life can only exist under certain conditions. These conditions exist near the surface of the earth in a thin region called the *biosphere*.

Biology can be divided into two basic groups, the study of plants, called *botany*, and the study of animals, called *zoology*. This book deals with the study of animals.

Six hundred years before Christ, a theory was developed that all living things originally came from water. One hundred years later, a Greek named Hippocrates made such amazing discoveries in the study of health that he is now called the "father of medicine." In early 1600, an English doctor discovered that blood circulates through the body. A French chemist, in the late 1800s discovered that germs caused disease. Nearly a half century ago, scientists in almost every field of biololgy began studying the ways that atomic radiation affects living plants and animals.

As equipment and instruments become more advanced, scientists can probe deeper into this curious phenomenon called life. An exciting future in this field is just waiting for anyone with a strong desire and the proper education. The following experiments will provide an introduction into the study of animal biology. Be sure to read the *Symbols Used in This Book* section that follows before you begin any experiments. It warns you of all the safety precautions you should consider before you begin a project and whether or not you should have a teacher, parent, or other adult help you.

Completely read through a project before you begin to be sure you understand the experiment and you have all of the materials you'll need. Each experiment has a materials list and easy, step-by-step instructions with illustrations to help you.

Although you will want to pick a project that interests you, you might want to do the experiments in order. It isn't necessary, but some of the principles you learn in the first few experiments will provide you with some basic understanding of biology and help you do later experiments.

Finally, keep safety in mind, and you are sure to hve a rewarding first experience in the exciting world of biology.

Symbols Used in This Book

Many of the experiments used in this book require the use of insects, knives, pins, and wire. It is recommended that a parent or teacher supervise young children and instruct them.

All of the experients in this book can be done safely, but young children should be instructed to respect the lives of small animals and insects and the hazards associated with carelessness. The following symbol is used throughout the book for you to use as a guide to what children might be able to do independently, and what they *should not do* wihtout adult supervision. Keep in mind that some children might not be mature enough to do any of the experiments wihtout adult help, and that these symbols should be used as a guide only and do not replace good judgment of parents or teachers.

 Materials or tools used in this experiment could be dangerous in young hands. Adult supervision is recommended. Children should be instructed on the care and handling of sharp tools or combustible or toxic materials and how to protect surfaces.

1

Parts of an Insect

Materials
DEAD INSECT (ANT)
MAGNIFYING GLASS

Examine the ant under the magnifying glass and notice it has six legs (Fig. 1-1). Look closely at the three parts of the jointed body. All mature insects have six legs and a jointed body. Creatures such as spiders, mites, ticks, and centipedes are not true insects.

The body is divided into three parts: the head, the middle body or *thorax*, and the abdomen (Fig. 1-2). The head contains its brain, its feelers or antennae, its eyes, and its mouth. The middle body contains the motor parts. It holds the main muscles that are used for walking, swimming, or flying. The legs, and any wings, are always connected to the middle body. The abdomen, at the rear of the insect, holds the digestive, reproductive, and other organs.

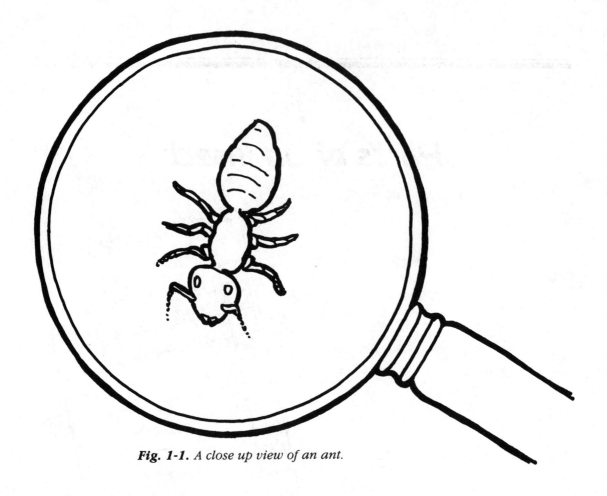

Fig. 1-1. *A close up view of an ant.*

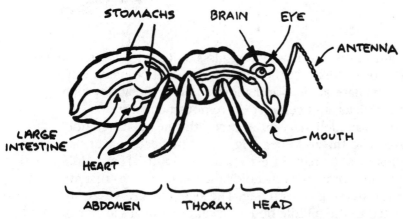

STOMACHS BRAIN EYE

ANTENNA

LARGE
INTESTINE

HEART

MOUTH

ABDOMEN THORAX HEAD

Fig. 1-2. *The body is made up of three parts.*

The outer body of an insect is made of a tough or horny material. This acts like a suit of armor and forms an outside skeleton. Insects have no internal framework of bones like we have. For an insect to grow, it must shed its outer skeleton and get a new and larger one.

The blood of an insect is normally yellowish, greenish, or colorless. It is pumped by the pulsating part of a tube-shaped blood vessel that extends the length of the body. This pumping part, called the *heart*, is located in the abdomen.

Insects have no lungs. They take in oxygen through small openings along the side of the body. All insects are coldblooded. This means that their body temperatures are about the same as their surroundings. Because of this, their activity depends a great deal on the temperature. Insects are more active on warm days.

2
Collecting Insects

Materials

- NETTING MATERIAL (CHEESECLOTH)
- WIRE (FROM CLOTHES HANGER)
- OLD BROOM HANDLE
- TAPE (FRICTION OR DUCT)

You can purchase a collecting net at some hobby stores (about $6.00 or $7.00), or you can make your own out of netting material. Bend the wire into a loop about 12 or 14 inches in diameter. Form the loop in the middle of the wire. Leave the ends of the wire bent down to fasten to the broom handle (Fig. 2-1). Tape the wire ends securely to the end of the broom handle (Fig. 2-2). You may need adult help to form a sock about 2 feet long from the netting material and use tape to fasten it to the wire loop (Fig. 2-3).

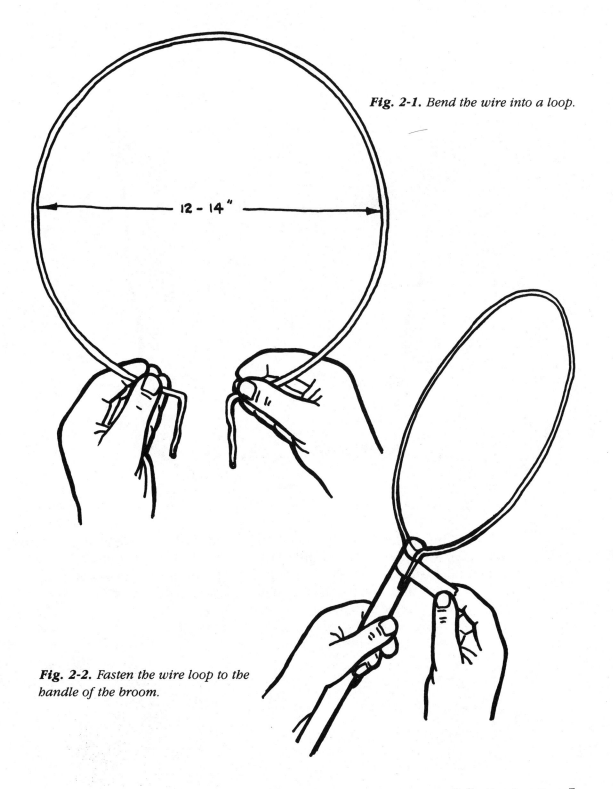

Fig. 2-1. Bend the wire into a loop.

12 - 14 "

Fig. 2-2. Fasten the wire loop to the handle of the broom.

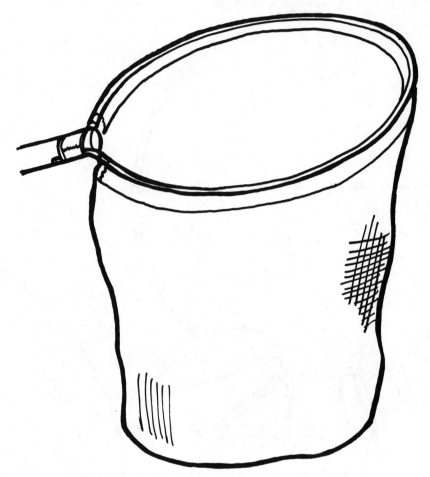

Fig. 2-3. *Attach the cheesecloth to the wire loop.*

Hold the net by the handle and swing it so that the net billows out. After you have caught an insect in the net, quickly rotate the wire loop to close the open end (Fig. 2-4). This traps the insect inside. You should now be able to transfer it to a jar. Be careful. Delicate wings are easily damaged. Be sure to avoid bees, wasps, and other stinging insects until you have a lot of experience.

Fig. 2-4. *Twist the handle to close off the net.*

3
A Jar For Killing Insects

Materials

- WIDE MOUTH GLASS JAR WITH LID
- COTTON
- FINGERNAIL POLISH REMOVER OR COMMERCIAL INSECTICIDE
- SMALL PIECE OF SCREEN WIRE

Place a layer of cotton in the bottom of the jar. Cut the screen wire that is cut to fit the inside of the jar and lay it on top of the cotton (Fig. 3-1). Pour some nail polish remover over the cotton until the cotton is saturated (Fig. 3-2). Drop the insect in the jar and quickly screw the lid in place (Fig. 3-3). The fumes from the nail polish remover should kill the insect within a few minutes.

This experiment should be done to study the insects. The killing of any living organism should be done with much consideration.

Fig. 3-1. *Place the wire screen on top of the cotton.*

Fig. 3-2. *Saturate the cotton with nail polish remover.*

Fig. 3-3. *The lid will keep the fumes inside the jar.*

4

Collecting Crawling Insects

Materials

- WIDE MOUTH GLASS JAR
- BOARD OR ROCK
- SHOVEL

Dig a small hole in the ground the size of the jar. Set the jar in the ground so that the rim is just below ground level. Fill in the area around the jar with dirt (Fig. 4-1). Place the board over the hole so that the board rests on the ground and not on the rim of the jar (Fig. 4-2). Insects like to hide under boards and rocks. When they fall into the jar, the slick sides prevent them from crawling back out. Check your trap every day and remove it when you are through collecting so no insects will die needlessly.

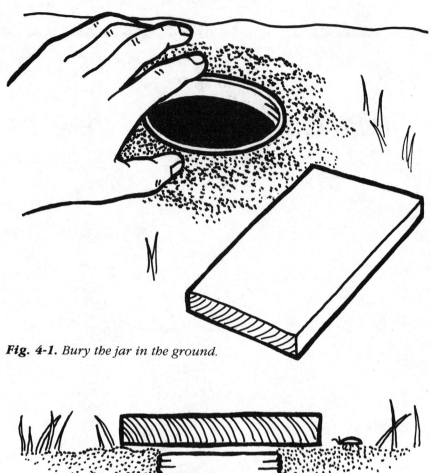

Fig. 4-1. *Bury the jar in the ground.*

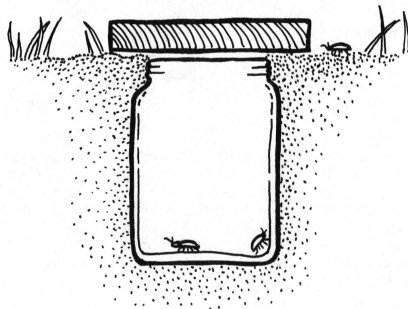

Fig. 4-2. *Place the board over the jar.*

Be very careful. Use long tweezers or forceps when picking up insects (Fig. 4-3). Many insects can bite or sting. Some insects, like scorpions, should be avoided altogether or killed while they are still in the trap.

Fig. 4-3. *Use tweezers to pick up the insects.*

5
A Jar for Relaxing Insects

Materials

- WIDE MOUTH GLASS JAR WITH LID
- COTTON
- WIRE SCREEN
- WATER

Place a layer of cotton in the bottom of the jar (Fig. 5-1) and put the wire screen on top, the same as the jar for studying dead insects. Only this time, soak the cotton with water (Fig. 5-2). When you find an insect that is already dead, place it in the jar (Fig. 5-3), replace the lid and let it set overnight (Fig. 5-4). The high humidity in the jar will relax the wings of butterflies, dragonflies, and other insects with large delicate wings.

Fig. 5-1. *Place cotton in the bottom of the jar.*

Fig. 5-2. *Saturate the cotton with water.*

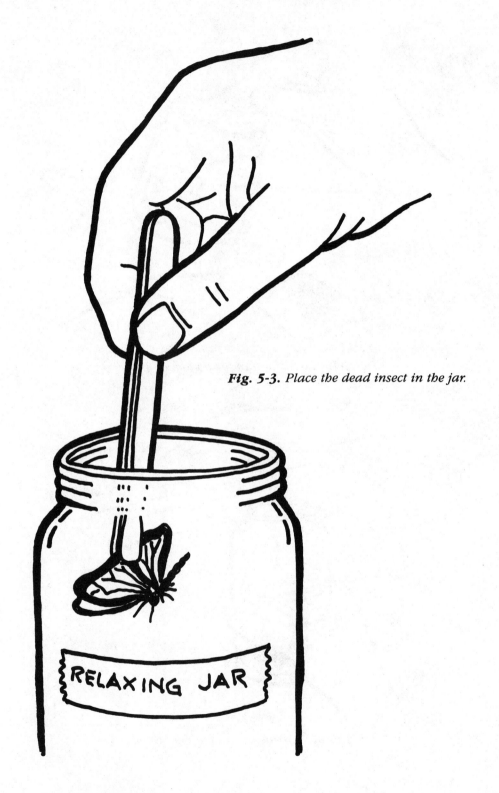

Fig. 5-3. *Place the dead insect in the jar.*

Fig. 5-4. *Let the jar set overnight.*

6

Making an Insect Spreading Board

Materials

- WOODEN BASE
- 2 PIECES OF HEAVY CARDBOARD
- 8 THUMBTACKS
- 4 PINS
- 2 NARROW STRIPS OF PAPER

Carefully cut the cardboard the size of the wings of the insect. Use the thumbtacks to fasten the pieces of cardboard to the wooden base (Fig. 6-1). Position the cardboard pieces side by side, and separate them by a space the size of the body of the insect. Place the body in this space, and spread the wings over the cardboard. Use the strips of paper that are the size of the wings of the insect and the pins (Fig. 6-2) to hold the wings in place until they dry in an open position (Fig. 6-3).

Fig. 6-1. *Use thumbtacks to hold the cardboard in place.*

Fig. 6-2. *Use paper strips and pins to hold the wings in place.*

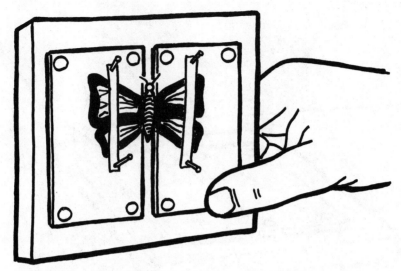

Fig. 6-3. *Let the insect dry with the wings in an open position.*

7

Mounting Insects

Materials

DEAD INSECTS

PINS

CARDBOARD

Identify and record each insect (Fig. 7-1). Carefully push the pin through the middle body (thorax) of the dead insect (Fig. 7-2). The abdomen might not be firm enough to hold the insect in a lifelike position. Stick the pin upright in the cardboard base. This allows the underside, as well as the top, of the insect to be examined (Fig. 7-3).

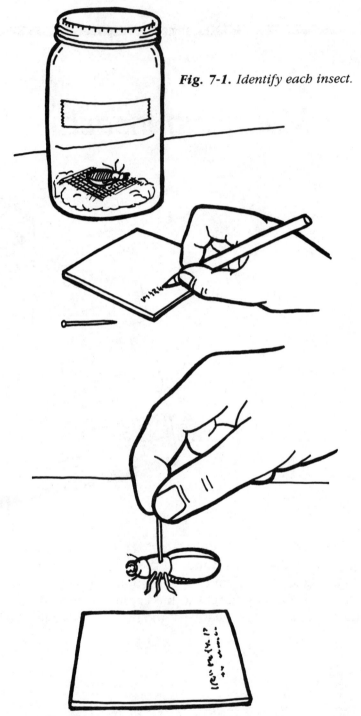

Fig. 7-1. Identify each insect.

Fig. 7-2. Push the pin through the middle part of the insect.

Fig. 7-3. *The top and the bottom of the insect can be examined.*

8
Starting an Ant Colony

Materials

- QUART MAYONNAISE JAR WITH LID
- 8- OR 10- OUNCE JELLY JAR WITH LID
- SOIL
- DARK CLOTH
- TROWEL OR SMALL SHOVEL
- WHITE CLOTH, 4 SQ. FT.
- STRING

Materials

- TWEEZERS OR FORCEPS
- ANTS

Find a nest under logs or rocks. Notice the kind of food the ants are bringing in. You will have to provide their food. Some ants are meat eaters, while others feed largely on plants. Use the shovel and carefully cut around the nest in about a 16-inch circle (Fig. 8-1). Pry up this mound of dirt, and place it and the ants on the white cloth. Be careful when working with ants since some small insects can sting or bite. Examine the contents until you locate the queen (Fig. 8-2). She should be larger and shinier than the rest of the ants. You also should see ants who are scurrying around carrying whitish-colored ant pupae and shinier objects called *ant larvae*. The larvae are hatched from the eggs and shed their skins several times before they become pupae.

Fig. 8-1. *Use a shovel to dig out the nest.*

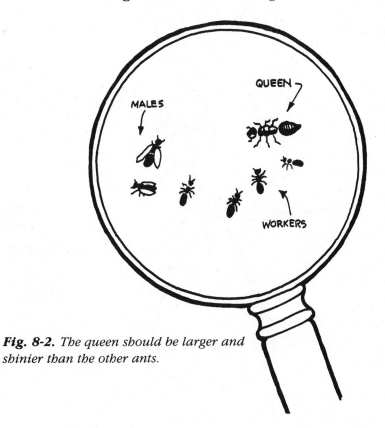

Fig. 8-2. *The queen should be larger and shinier than the other ants.*

Pupae are ants who are immobile and are in the nonfeeding transformation stage before becoming adults. Collect about three dozen of these pupae and larvae along with about the same number of adult ants. Collect the queen because she produces the eggs for the new generation. Fold the cloth into a bag and tie it with the string (Fig. 8-3). Take it home to transfer the ants and soil to the new nest.

Fig. 8-3. *Collect the ants in the cloth bag.*

Make sure the jars are clean and dry. Put the lid on the smaller jar, and place it inside the larger jar (Fig. 8-4). Try to keep the smaller jar in the center and fill the space between the two jars with the soil from the nest. A paper funnel can be used to transfer ants and soil (Fig. 8-5). Fill the space to within a couple of inches of the top. Punch a few holes in the lid to let in air. Cover the jar with the dark cloth for a couple of weeks to let the ants get settled and start to tunnel (Fig. 8-6). Remove the cover for observations. Keep a small piece of damp sponge in the nest for moisture (Fig. 8-7), and try to determine what kind of food your ants prefer.

Fig. 8-4. *Place the smaller jar inside the larger one.*

Fig. 8-5. *Use a paper funnel to transfer the ants and the soil.*

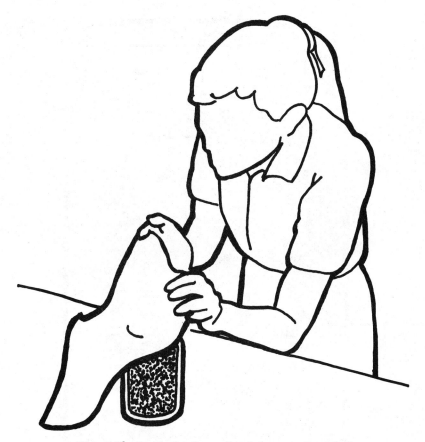

Fig. 8-6. *Cover the jar to let the ants get settled.*

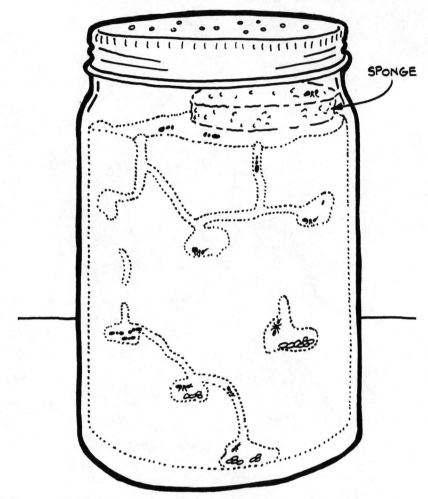

SPONGE

Fig. 8-7. *A damp sponge will keep moisture in the jar.*

9

From a Caterpillar to a Butterfly or Moth

Materials

CATERPILLAR
FRESH LEAVES
WATER
CAGE

Collect a few caterpillars and the leaves on which they are feeding (Fig. 9-1). Place them in the cage, and keep them supplied with fresh leaves (Fig. 9-2). When the caterpillar has finished growing, it will hang by its tail from a safe location under a board or leaf and build itself a protective cover (Fig. 9-3)—a cocoon for a moth and a chrysalis, the hard-shelled pupa, for a butterfly. The cage should be placed outside through the winter. In the spring, sprinkle the leaves with water, about once a week and the adults will emerge. Provide them with fresh leaves, and set them free when you have made your observations (Fig. 9-4).

Fig. 9-1. *Collect the caterpillars and the leaves they are feeding on.*

Fig. 9-2. *Keep the caterpillars supplied with fresh leaves.*

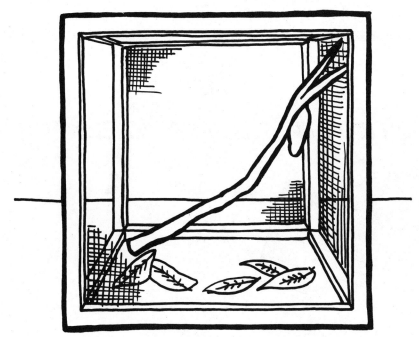

Fig. 9-3. *The caterpillar will build a cocoon.*

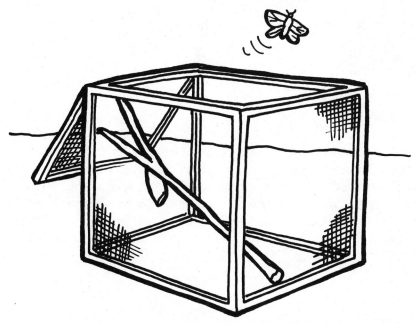

Fig. 9-4. *Set them free when you have finished your experiment.*

10
From a Tadpole to a Frog

Materials

- AQUARIUM
- WATER
- SAND
- A FEW TADPOLES
- WATER PLANTS
- ALGAE-COVERED ROCKS FROM NEARBY POND
- BITS OF HARD-BOILED EGG
- MAGNIFYING GLASS

Build a small beach of sand at one end of your aquarium (Fig. 10-1). Add a few inches of water, a couple of water plants, and a few algae-covered rocks. Drop in about 6 or 8 tadpoles (Fig. 10-2). Do not put the aquarium in direct sunlight. Warm water will kill the tadpoles. Tadpoles feed on the tiny algae that grow on underwater rocks and the stems of water plants. Older tadpoles can be fed bits of a hard-boiled egg.

Fig. 10-1. *Make a sandy beach at one end of your aquarium.*

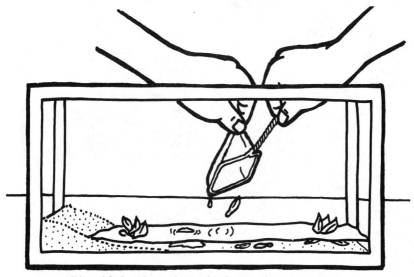

Fig. 10-2. *Place the tadpoles in the aquarium.*

Use the magnifying glass to monitor the changes as the tadpoles grow. The complete change can take a few months, or in the case of the bullfrog species, up to two years, but they will gradually grow legs, lose their tail, and turn into adult frogs (Fig. 10-3).

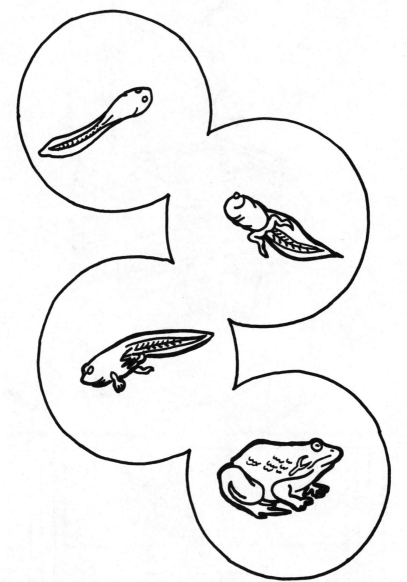

Fig. 10-3. *The tadpole will slowly grow legs, lose its tail, and become an adult frog.*

11
Frogs in Hibernation

Materials

AQUARIUM
WATER
DIRT
WIRE SCREEN
FROG

Construct a semi-aquatic aquarium by building a mud bank leading up to a small hill of dirt at one end, and a small pool of water in the other end (Fig. 11-1). Try to make it a natural surrounding. Feed your frog live insects such as small bugs and flies. Notice the breathing of the frog. This can be seen in the rapid pulsing of its throat. In the fall of the year, place the aquarium outside in the cold for several hours (Fig. 11-2). Look at the frog's throat. You should see that its breathing has slowed, and the frog appears sluggish. It

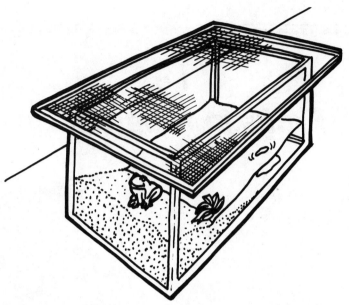

Fig. 11-1. *Have a small hill of dirt at one end of the aquarium and a small pool of water at the other end.*

Fig. 11-2. *When winter comes, place the aquarium outside in the cold for a few hours.*

will start to burrow into the mud bank and go into hibernation (Fig. 11-3). If you have mild winters, you might try scattering ice cubes inside the aquarium. This also can cause the frog to go into hibernation. At this time, frogs go into a long sleep until the warmth of spring wakes them up.

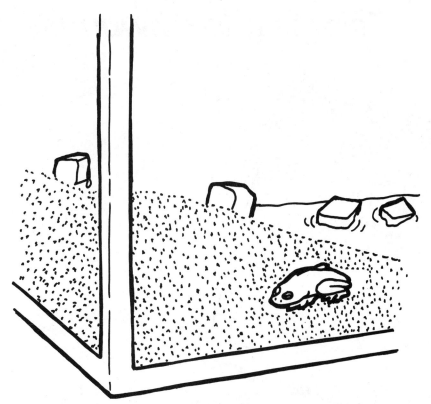

Fig. 11-3. *The frog will burrow into the dirt to hibernate.*

12
Collecting Earthworms

Materials

- COFFEE CAN
- SHOVEL
- GARDEN SOIL OR WARM, MOIST SOIL
- MAGNIFYING GLASS

Earthworms like to live in soil that is rich in humus and decaying plant or animal material. Push the shovel deep into this type of soil, and turn it upside down. This should uncover the worms. Fill the can with this dirt and add worms as you find them (Fig. 12-1). Earthworms also can be found on top of the ground and sidewalks after a rainstorm. They come to the surface to get air because the soaking rain water forces out the air in the soil. Examine the worms with the magnifying glass (Fig. 12-2). You will see that they have a long slender body that is covered with a slimy fluid. You also can see that the worm is divided into segments, or rings, and is reddish brown in color. The earthworm has no eyes, but there is a pair of

Fig. 12-1. *Place the worms in the can of dirt.*

Fig. 12-2. *A close-up view of a worm.*

spots on each segment that is sensitive to light. Tiny bristles underneath and on each side of its body help the worm pull itself along by contracting its muscles (Fig. 12-3). Earthworms are some of the most important animals on earth. They keep the ground porous. This helps the growth of plants.

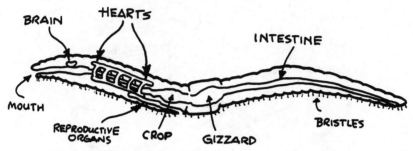

Fig. 12-3. Tiny bristles help the worm pull itself along.

13

Keeping Earthworms

Materials
- LARGE WIDE MOUTH JAR, OR OLD AQUARIUM
- RICH SOIL
- LEAF MOLD
- SAND
- WATER
- VEGETABLE LEAVES AND CORNMEAL, OR OATMEAL
- DARK CLOTH

Materials
- EARTHWORMS

Fill the jar with layers of sand, leaf mold, and soil. Sprinkle each layer with a little water as you fill the jar. Place a small handful of cornmeal or oatmeal on the top of the last layer, and add a few small pieces of a vegetable leaf (Fig. 13-1). Place several earthworms in the jar (Fig. 13-2), and cover it with the dark cloth (Fig. 13-3). Let it set for about a week. This will make the worms feel at home and encourage them to tunnel near the sides of the jar (Fig. 13-4). Keep the soil moist, and add food about twice a week.

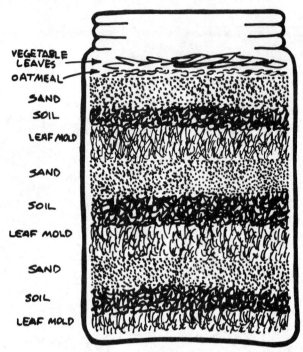

VEGETABLE LEAVES
OATMEAL
SAND
SOIL
LEAF MOLD
SAND
SOIL
LEAF MOLD
SAND
SOIL
LEAF MOLD

Fig. 13-1. *Place a few small pieces of a vegetable leaf on top.*

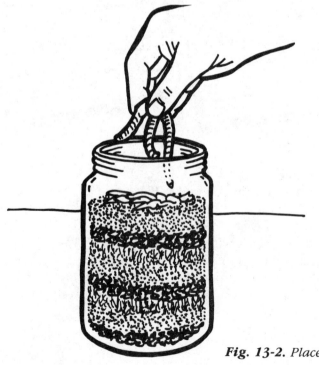

Fig. 13-2. *Place the worms in the jar.*

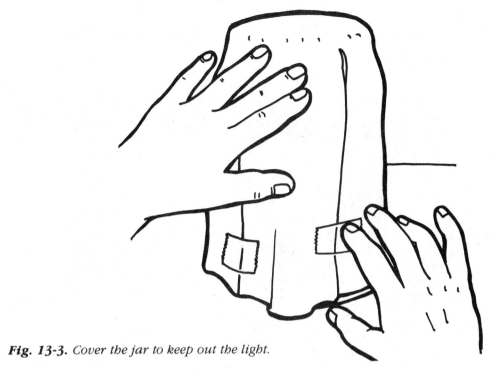

Fig. 13-3. *Cover the jar to keep out the light.*

Fig. 13-4. *The worms should tunnel near the sides of the jar.*

14
Keeping a Turtle

Materials

TURTLE
TERRARIUM
COARSE SAND
DIRT OR FINE SAND

It is against the law in some places to take turtles from the wild. Small turtles can often be found in pet stores. Your terrarium should be as close as possible to the natural habitat of the turtle you buy. This includes the temperature and humidity. You can use an old aquarium or make a terrarium from a cardboard or wooden box. Cut out one side of the box and glue in a transparent piece of plastic (Fig. 14-1). Water must be kept in a pan or bowl. It can be sunk in the soil to simulate a small pond. Pour a layer of coarse sand in the bottom of your terrarium. Add a layer of dirt, or fine sand, depending on the type of turtle you have (Fig. 14-2). Plants of that

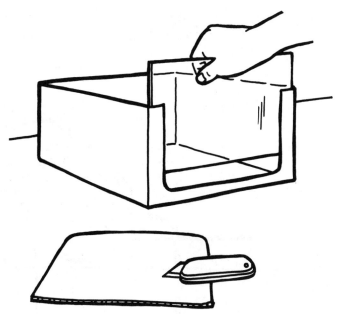

Fig. 14-1. *Glue a piece of plastic in one end.*

Fig. 14-2. *Add a layer of dirt or sand.*

habitat can be added (Fig. 14-3). Sprinkle the soil and plants with water, daily if the turtles are used to moisture, or only once a week if it is a desert terrarium. Some turtles will eat bits of fruit and vegetables. Others prefer insects and pieces of meat, such as liver.

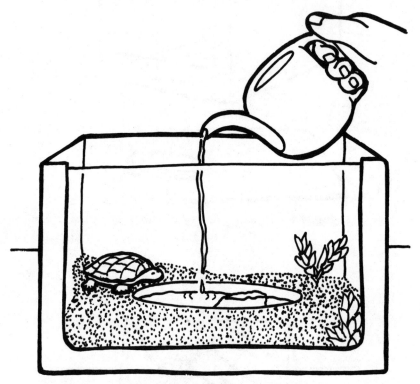

Fig. 14-3. *Add plants and fresh water to your terrarium.*

15
Parts of a Fish

Look at Fig. 15-1 and notice the different parts of the fish's body. The fish was the first animal with a backbone, and they are in greater numbers than any other animal with a backbone. A fish breathes with gills instead of lungs. Gills contain blood vessels that absorb oxygen through the thin membranes in the gills. Fish take in oxygen and give off carbon dioxide. In place of arms and legs, they have two pairs of fins; the pectoral fins, just behind the head, operate like our arms, and the pelvic fins, located on the lower part of the body, correspond to our legs. The remaining fins serve as keels and rudders (Fig. 15-1). Fish are coldblooded and their body

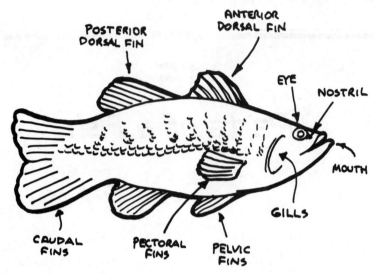

Fig. 15-1. *Parts of a fish's body.*

temperature is about the same as the water in which they live. Their internal organs (brain, nerves, skeleton, and muscles), are similar to other backboned animals (Fig. 15-2). Most fish, however, depend heavily on a sense of smell and a special sense in the lateral line. This is a row of tubes and pores over a nerve that runs along the side of the fish's body. This sense organ is able to detect the slightest of vibrations. There are many different kinds of fish who live in the oceans, lakes, and streams all over the world. Their size, shape, and the way they live depends on the particular place in which they live.

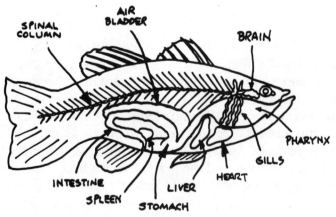

Fig. 15-2. *An inside look at a fish.*

16
Raising Guppies

Materials

- LARGE BOWL OR AN AQUARIUM
- WATER
- CLEAN SAND OR FINE GRAVEL
- WATER PLANTS
- GUPPIES
- HATCHING BOWL

Place a layer of sand in the bottom of the aquarium (Fig. 16-1), and add plants (Fig. 16-2), or other suitable objects, to provide hiding places for the young. The mother guppy will eat her young. Add water at the rate of one gallon for every pair of guppies. Guppies like warm water, between 70 and 100° Fahrenheit (Fig. 16-3). Feed your guppies commercial fish food such as brine shrimp, but be careful not to overfeed. It may take about a month for the new guppies to appear, but when the female is about to produce her young, separate

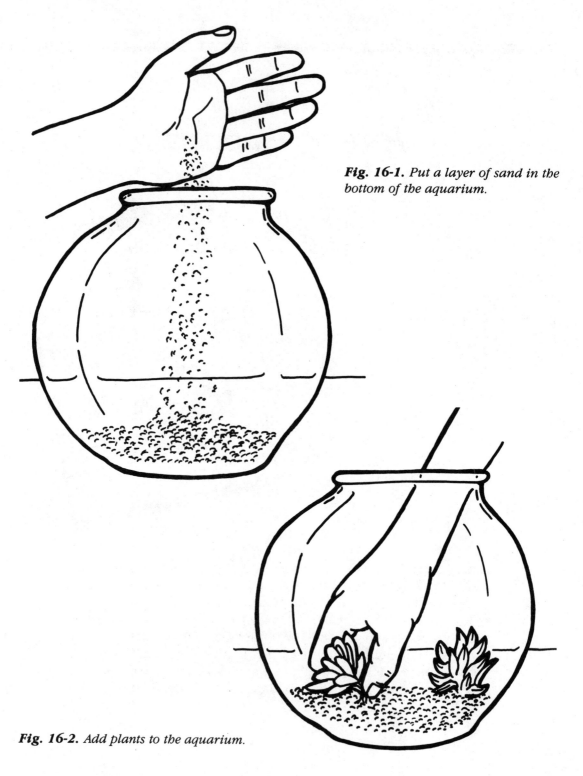

Fig. 16-1. *Put a layer of sand in the bottom of the aquarium.*

Fig. 16-2. *Add plants to the aquarium.*

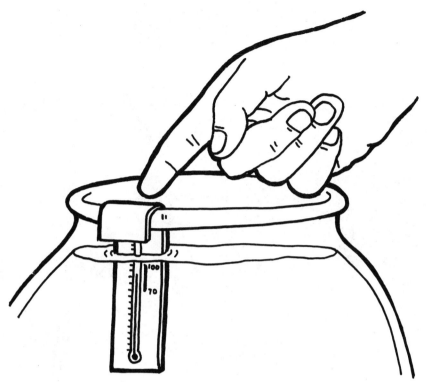

Fig. 16-3. *Guppies prefer warm water.*

her from the rest of the fish. Place her in a separate container (Fig. 16-4). As soon as the guppies are born, return the mother to the aquarium. Otherwise, she will quickly devour the young. When the young guppies get larger, place them in the aquarium with the rest of the fish.

Fig. 16-4. *Separate the mother from the baby guppies.*

17
Parts of a Bird

Look at the illustration and notice the different parts of a bird (Fig. 17-1). There are many different kinds of birds, and they vary in size and shape. But all their bodies are similar. The skeleton of a bird is specifically designed for flying. The bones are thin and small, but they still do their job. The longer bones are hollow to keep down weight (Fig. 17-2). The bones fit together in such a way that makes the skeleton a rigid framework except, for the neck. It is flexible and allows the bird to reach any part of its body with its beak. A little sparrow has twice as many bones in its neck as a giraffe. More than half of the birds's weight is made up of muscles. The largest

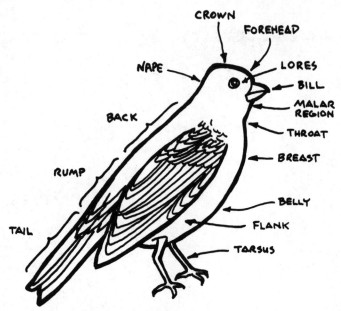

Fig. 17-1. *Different parts of a bird.*

Fig. 17-2. *Birds have hollow bones to keep down weight.*

are the muscles in its breast that operate the wings. Feathers give the bird the ability to fly (Fig. 17-3). They streamline its body and maintain the body temperature. The larger feathers on the tip of the wing are the primary feathers. They are connected to bones that correspond to our hands. The secondary feathers, closer in to the body, are connected to bones that correspond to our forearms. These feathers open as the bird pulls its wings up and forward, then close when it pushes down and back against the air. Birds have excellent eyesight and hearing, but their sense of smell and taste are not as good. It is believed that the ancestors of birds were reptiles, because they have many of the same characteristics as reptiles (Fig. 17-4).

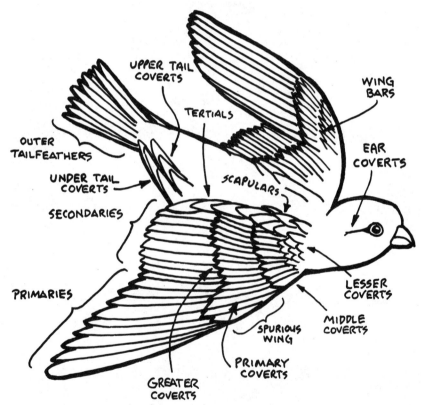

Fig. 17-3. *Feathers allow birds to fly.*

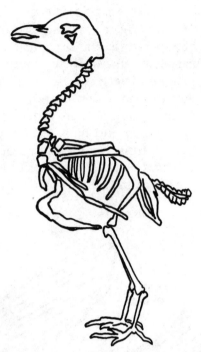

Fig. 17-4. *The ancestors of birds might have been reptiles.*

18
Studying and Identifying Birds

Materials
- NOTEBOOK AND PENCIL
- POCKET SIZE BIRD IDENTIFICATION BOOK
- BINOCULARS

Study pictures of birds and try to learn their names (Fig. 18-1). Look for birds in their natural surroundings such as trees, underbrush, and near water (Fig. 18-2). City parks can be a good place to start. It also helps to go with someone who already knows about birds. Zoos have live birds from other countries, and museums often have exhibits of stuffed birds in lifelike surroundings.

Birds are easily frightened, so it is important to move slowly and quietly. Dull-colored clothes will help keep you from being noticeable in woods or fields. You can hide near a nest, and wait for the birds to come and go. Birdbaths are good places to observe

Fig. 18-1. *Learn to identify birds in your area.*

Fig. 18-2. *Birds can be found in trees and bushes.*

birds who are drinking and bathing. First, notice the size and shape of the bird (Fig. 18-3). Look for colors and the patterns of the feathers (Fig. 18-4). Listen for their songs or calls, and notice the pattern of their flights (Fig. 18-5). Some birds soar, while others fly in jerky up and down flights. It will be easy to tell a sparrow from a robin, and in time, you will be able to identify many other varieties (Fig. 18-6).

Fig. 18-3. *Notice the body of the bird, its size and shape.*

Fig. 18-4. *Notice the color and patterns of the feathers.*

Fig. 18-5. *Humming birds can hover then dart off in any direction.*

Fig. 18-6. *Soon you will be able to identify the birds in your area.*

19

Building a Bird House

Materials

OLD UNPAINTED WOOD

DRILL

HAMMER AND NAILS

SAW

NESTING MATERIAL

The size and shape of the house depends on the type of bird. But weathered, unpainted wood is preferred over metal. Roofs should be sloped to allow the rain to run off. You might even drill a couple of small holes in the floor to let out any rain water that might get in. A few holes that are drilled in the walls, just under the roof overhang, will provide ventilation and help in cooling the inside (Fig. 19-1). Generally, the floor of the house should be about 5 × 5 inches, and walls about 8 to 10 inches high (Fig. 19-2). The hole for the entrance should be about 2 inches in diameter and in the upper half of the front wall (Fig. 19-3). The bird house can be mounted on a post or fastened to a tree, and should be from 6 to 15 feet above

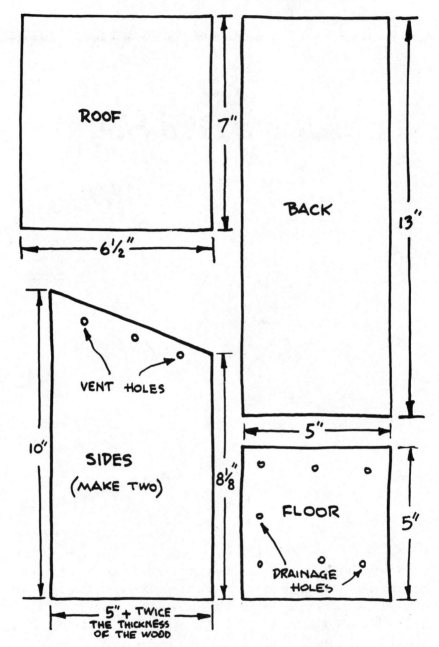

Fig. 19-1. *A pattern for a typical bird house.*

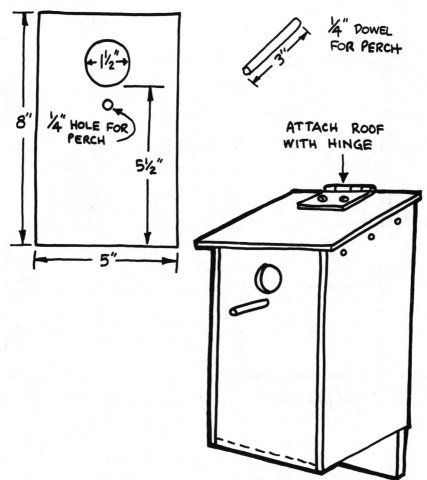

FRONT:

1½"

8"

¼" HOLE FOR PERCH

5½"

5"

¼" DOWEL FOR PERCH

3"

ATTACH ROOF WITH HINGE

Fig. 19-2. *A bird house with a hinged roof.*

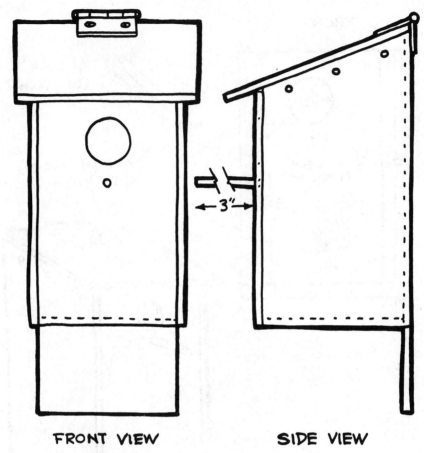

FRONT VIEW   **SIDE VIEW**

Fig. 19-3. *Front and side view of a bird house.*

the ground. Place a sheet of tin around the post or tree trunk to protect the birds from cats and squirrels. Early in the spring, place nesting material that can include yarn, pieces of rag, twigs, and bits of wood shavings on the ground close to the bird house. The nesting birds will find it and use what they need. Use the illustrations for a reference and notice that a robin likes an open nesting shelf (Fig. 19-4), while purple martins prefer apartment living (Fig. 19-5).

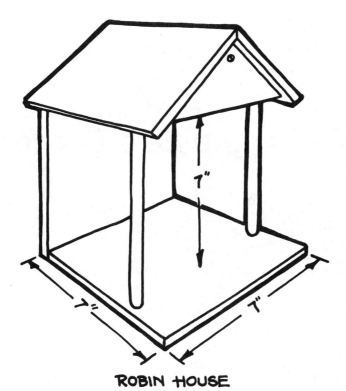

ROBIN HOUSE

Fig. 19-4. *Robins like an open house.*

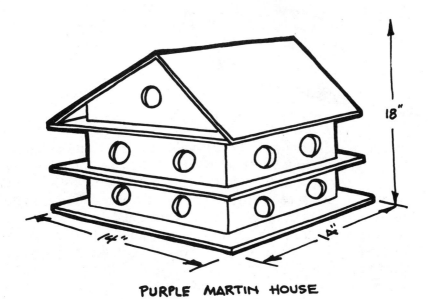

PURPLE MARTIN HOUSE

Fig. 19-5. *Purple martins prefer apartments.*

20
Building a Bird Feeder

A feeding tray is easy to make. All you need is a board about 12 inches long and about 12 inches wide. Add strips of wood around the edges to keep the food from falling off, and place it near a window (Fig. 20-1). Make sure the tray is out of reach of cats and other enemies of birds. A metal fence guard will discourage hungry cats (Fig. 20-2). You also can build a trolley feeder. Run a small rope, like a clothesline, from a window to a tree or post. Attach straps and pulleys to a feeding tray and use a string to pull it closer to the window as the birds lose their shyness (Fig. 20-3). You can add a

Fig. 20-1. *Place the feeding tray near a window.*

roof to your feeding tray to keep out the rain and snow (Fig. 20-4). A couple of holes that are drilled in the floor will let rain and snow drain out.

You can feed birds suet, or beef fat, and scraps of meat. Many birds like grains, bread crumbs, and crumpled dog biscuits. You also can use boiled potatoes, finely chopped hard boiled eggs, raw or boiled rice, and fruits. Just remember that if you give the birds too much food, they will become dependent on you and lose their self-reliance. If this happens, they will not forage for themselves, and in winter, if you're not there to feed them, they could freeze and die.

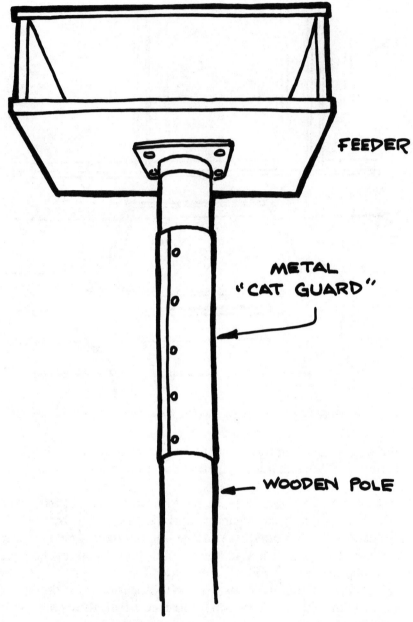

FEEDER

METAL
"CAT GUARD"

WOODEN POLE

Fig. 20-2. *Metal guards keep cats away.*

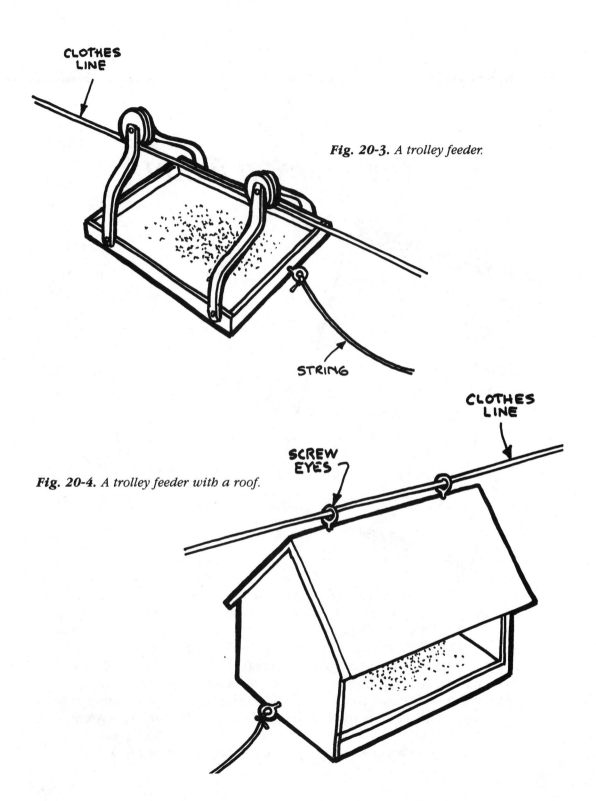

CLOTHES LINE

Fig. 20-3. *A trolley feeder.*

STRING

CLOTHES LINE

SCREW EYES

Fig. 20-4. *A trolley feeder with a roof.*

21

The Human Body

The human body can be thought of as containing seven systems: (1) the skeleton, or skeletal system is the framework of bones (Fig. 21-1); (2) the muscular system supports and moves the skeleton (Fig. 21-2); (3) digestive system supplies the blood with digested food to provide the body with energy (Fig. 21-3); (4) the circulatory system extends throughout the body sending blood that is carrying food and oxygen, and on the return trip, carries away nitrogen wastes and carbon dioxide (Fig. 21-4); (5) the urinary system removes nitrogen wastes from the blood (Fig. 21-5); (6) the respiratory system allows us to take in oxygen from the air and

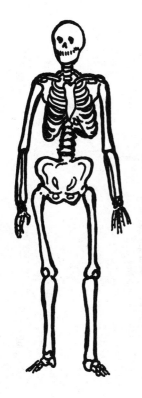

Fig. 21-1. *The human skeleton.*

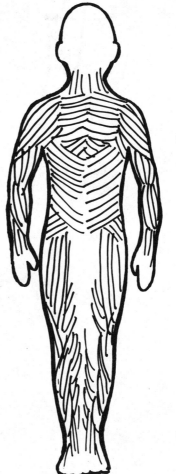

MUSCLES,
TENDONS
& LIGAMENTS

Fig. 21-2. *Muscles support the skeleton and make it move.*

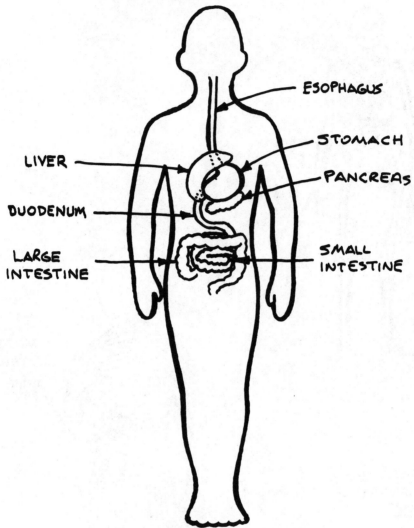

ESOPHAGUS

STOMACH

LIVER

PANCREAS

DUODENUM

LARGE
INTESTINE

SMALL
INTESTINE

Fig. 21-3. *The human digestive system.*

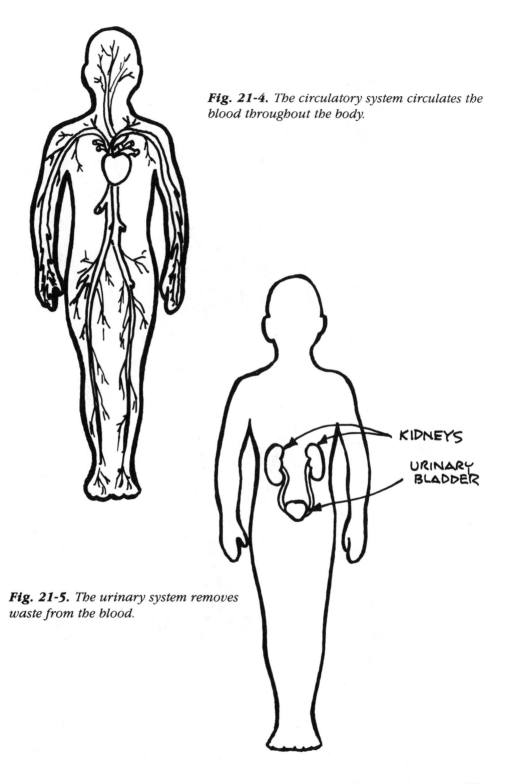

Fig. 21-4. The circulatory system circulates the blood throughout the body.

KIDNEYS

URINARY BLADDER

Fig. 21-5. The urinary system removes waste from the blood.

deliver it to our blood, and at the same time, remove carbon dioxide from the blood and release it back into the air (Fig. 21-6); and, (7) the nervous system is the system that carries messages between the brain and the organs and other parts of the body (Fig. 21-7).

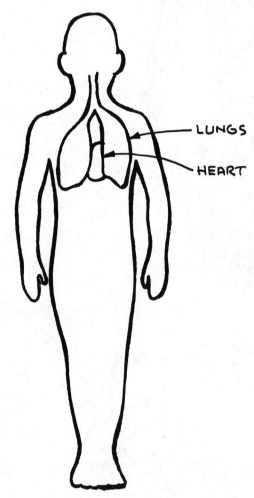

Fig. 21-6. *The respiratory system lets us take in oxygen and remove carbon dioxide from our blood.*

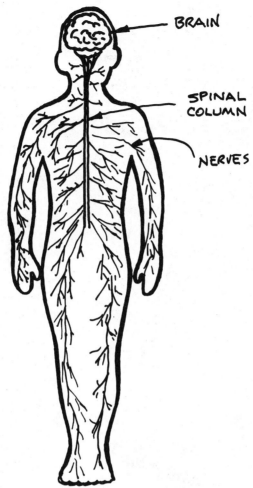

BRAIN

SPINAL
COLUMN

NERVES

Fig. 21-7. *The nervous system carries messages from the brain to all parts of the body.*

22

Taking Your Temperature

Materials

MERCURY THERMOMETER

ALCOHOL

First dip the thermometer in alcohol to kill any germs (Fig. 22-1). Grasp the top securely and shake the thermometer (Fig. 22-2). This sends the mercury to the bottom of the tube. Place the end of the thermometer under your tongue and carefully close your mouth (Fig. 22-3). Leave the thermometer in place for several minutes. Remove it and read the scale. It should be about 98.6°, or 37° C on a centigrade scale (Fig. 22-4). You also can take your temperature under your armpit, but it will read about one degree lower than your body temperature.

Fig. 22-1. *Clean the thermometer with alcohol.*

Fig. 22-2. *Shake the thermometer to lower the mercury in the tube.*

Fig. 22-3. *Place the thermometer under your tongue.*

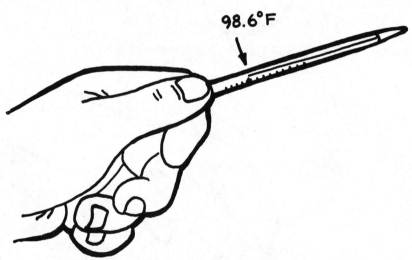

98.6°F

Fig. 22-4. *Normal body temperature is about 98.6°F.*

23

How Muscles Control Bones

Materials

- 2 PIECES OF WOOD
- DRILL
- NUT AND BOLT
- SCREW EYES AND HOOKS
- LONG, HEAVY RUBBER BAND
- HEAVY STRING OR CORD

Ask an adult to drill a hole in one end of each board (Fig. 23-1). The boards should be about 3×12 inches in length and $1/4$ inch thick. Fasten the boards together with the nut and bolt (Fig. 23-2). Don't tighten the nut too much. The connection should be free to bend. Attach the screw eyes and hooks as shown in Fig. 23-3, and thread the rubber band through the eyes and loop it over the hooks (Fig. 23-4). Next, thread the string through the eyes on top of the model, and fasten it to the hook. When you pull on the string, the arm will bend and when the string is released the arm will straighten (Fig. 23-5). A screw can be added as a stop to keep the arm from bending too far back.

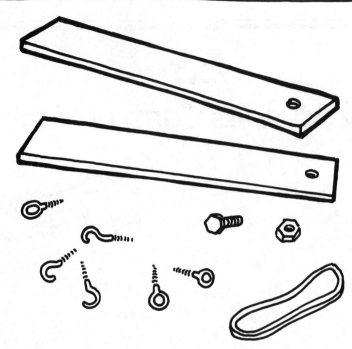

Fig. 23-1. *You need two boards with holes in one end to make the model.*

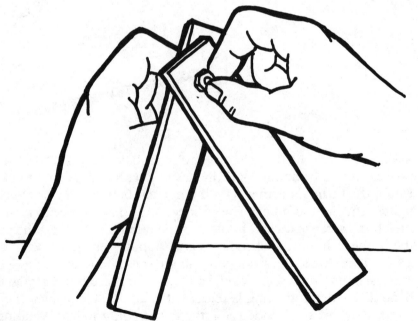

Fig. 23-2. *Fasten the boards together with a nut and a bolt.*

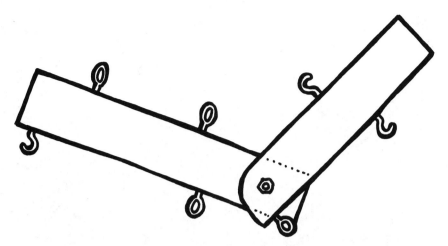

Fig. 23-3. *Attach the screw eyes and hooks to the boards.*

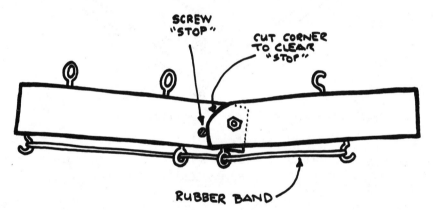

SCREW "STOP"

CUT CORNER TO CLEAR "STOP"

RUBBER BAND

Fig. 23-4. *Thread the rubber band through the screw eyes on the bottom of the boards.*

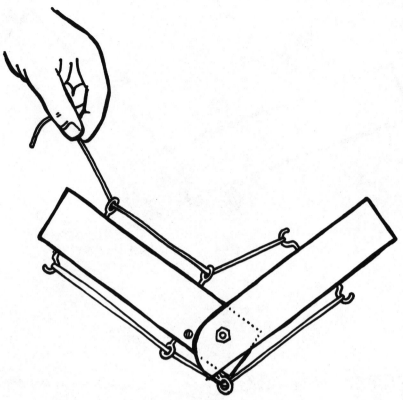

Fig. 23-5. *Pull the string on the top to move the arm.*

The model shows how muscles move bones. The string and rubber band represent the muscles, and the boards represent the bones.

24

The Mind and the Muscles

Materials

AN OPEN DOORWAY

Stand in the middle of the doorway and move your arms out until the back of each hand is against the sides of the opening (Fig. 24-1). Gradually begin pressing out as if you were trying to raise your arms. Continue trying to raise your arms for about 30 seconds. Stop and quickly move out of the opening. Your arms will rise by themselves (Fig. 24-2). The brain sent signals to the muscles to raise the arms. This signal was sent for a long enough period to put tension on the muscles. When you stepped out in the open, some of the tension was still there, and the arms began to rise.

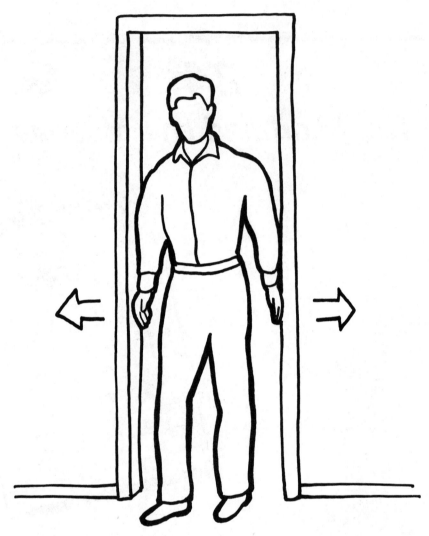

Fig. 24-1. *Press your hands against the opening in the door.*

Fig. 24-2. *Your arms will begin to rise themselves.*

25

How Our Lungs Work

Materials

- LARGE, CLEAR PLASTIC JAR
- CORK STOPPER WITH HOLE
- SMALL TUBE
- BALLOON
- PIECE OF BROKEN BALLOON
- STRING
- TAPE

Materials

- KNIFE

Carefully, cut the bottom out of the jar (Fig. 25-1). Next, insert the tube through the cork, and press it into the top of the jar (Fig. 25-2). Use string to fasten the balloon to the tube (Fig. 25-3). Tie a knot in the center of the piece of broken balloon to serve as a handle, then stretch the piece over the opening in the bottom of the jar, leaving the knot on the outside. Hold it in place with the string. Use tape to seal the edges to the jar (Fig. 25-4). The balloon will represent the lungs and the stretched cover over the bottom will represent the large muscle under the lungs (the diaphragm) that helps us breathe.

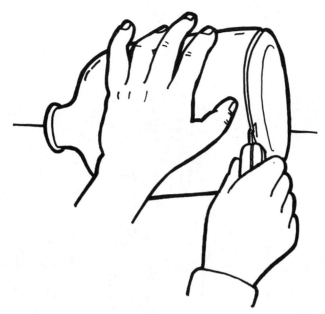

Fig. 25-1. *Carefully cut the bottom from the plastic jar.*

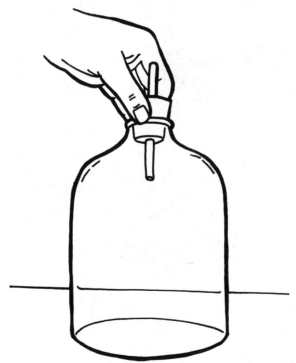

Fig. 25-2. *Press the cork with the tube into the opening.*

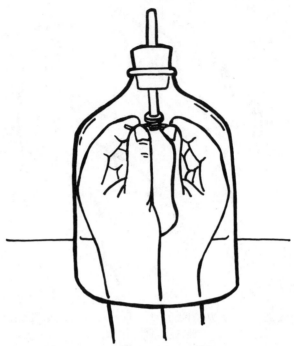

Fig. 25-3. *Tie the balloon to the end of the tube.*

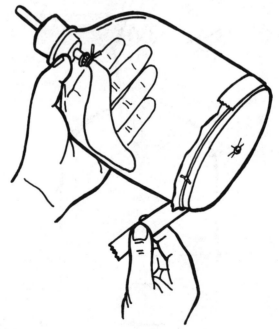

Fig. 25-4. *Use tape to seal the edges of the broken balloon.*

There are no muscles in the lungs. Hold the knot and slowly push
in on the diaphragm, and then gradually pull back out (Fig. 25-5).
Notice how the balloon fills with air and then deflates. This is how
we breathe.

Fig. 25-5. *Notice the balloon as you push in and pull out on the bottom.*

26
How Much Air Do the Lungs Hold

Materials

CLEAR JAR
RUBBER TUBING
CRAYON MARKER
QUART MEASURING JAR
WATER
SINK

Fill the sink with water and submerge the jar, about ½ gallon in size, in the water with the open end up (Fig. 26-1), completely filling the jar with water. Try to get all of the air out of the jar. Turn the jar upside down, still under water. Insert one end of the rubber tube, which should be about 2 feet long, into the jar, leaving the other end above the surface. Take a normal breath and breathe out into the free end of the rubber tube (Fig. 26-2). You want to capture your breath in the jar. Your breath will push some of the water out of the jar. Use the crayon to mark the water level on the jar (Fig. 26-3). Empty the jar and place it upright on a table. Fill the

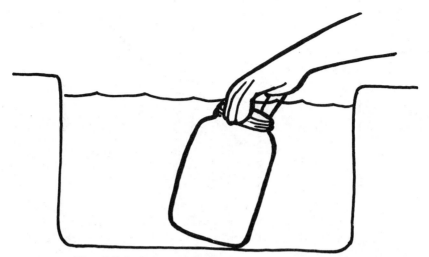

Fig. 26-1. *Submerge the jar in the sink of water.*

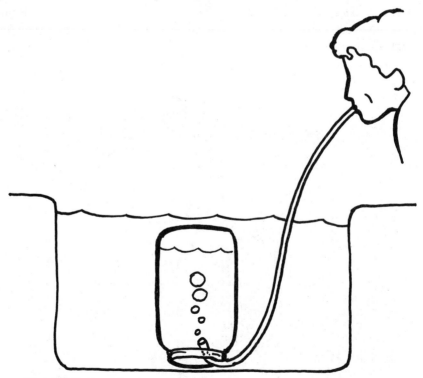

Fig. 26-2. *Breathe into the tube to capture your breath in the jar.*

Fig. 26-3. Use a crayon to mark the water level on the jar.

measuring jar with water, and pour it into the larger jar (Fig. 26-4). Measure the amount of water it takes to bring the water up to the mark. This represents the approximate volume of air you breathe in and out with each breath. That is almost 60 cubic inches of air for each quart of water.

Fig. 26-4. The amount of water represents the volume of air in your breath.

27

Why We Must Breathe

Try holding your breath for a few seconds. Notice how your body tries to tell you something. Soon you will have to take a deep breath. When we breathe, we take in oxygen (Fig. 27-1) and exhale carbon dioxide (Fig. 27-2). When you held your breath, your body sensed a reduced level of oxygen in your blood and began sending out signals that demand that you breathe (Fig. 27-3). Your body also senses the thinner air when you are hiking at high altitudes in the mountains. This causes your heart to do more work and increases your rate of breathing.

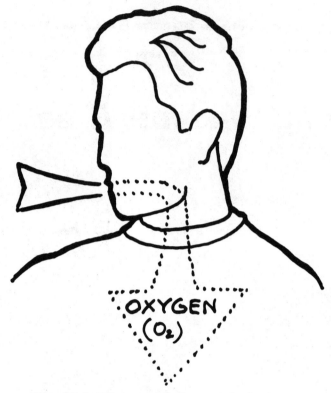

Fig. 27-1. *When we inhale, we take in oxygen.*

Fig. 27-2. *When we exhale, we exhale carbon dioxide.*

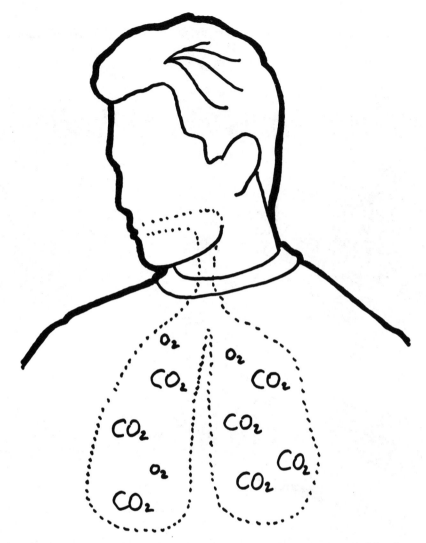

Fig. 27-3. *Our bodies sense the amount of oxygen in our blood.*

28

Watching Your Pulse

Materials

WOODEN MATCH

THUMBTACK

Mount the wooden match upright on the point of the thumbtack (Fig. 28-1). Place your finger on your wrist, and find the place where you can feel your pulse (Fig. 28-2). Lay your arm, with the wrist up, on a table or other solid object. Position the head of the thumbtack on the spot where you felt your pulse, and hold your arm still (Fig. 28-3). You should see a slight but steady movement at the top of the match. This movement reflects the pulsing of your blood through the artery in your wrist.

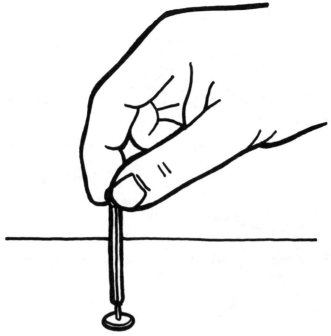

Fig. 28-1. *Press the wooden match onto the point of the thumbtack.*

Fig. 28-2. *Locate the pulse in your wrist.*

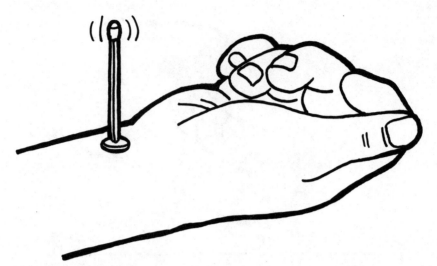

Fig. 28-3. *Place the match and thumbtack on the spot where you felt your pulse.*

29

How Our Blood Circulates

Let your arm hang down limp for several seconds (Fig. 29-1). Look closely at the top of your hand. You should see a few blue lines just under the skin (Fig. 29-2). These are the blood veins. Press the tip of your finger down on one of the veins that are near the wrist. Push your finger along the vein toward the knuckles (Fig. 29-3). Notice how the vein seems to disappear. Release your finger and the vein instantly fills back up. The veins have valves in them that allow the blood to flow in one direction only; to the heart (Fig. 29-4). Blood circulates throughout our body through a system of tubes. The larger tubes, some as big as your thumb, are called

Fig. 29-1. *Let your arm hang limp for a few seconds.*

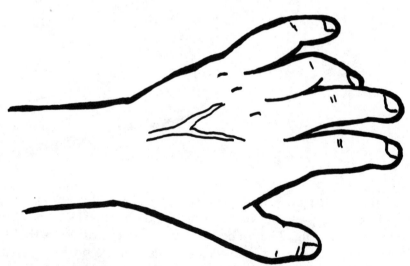

Fig. 29-2. *You should be able to see blood veins on the top of your hand.*

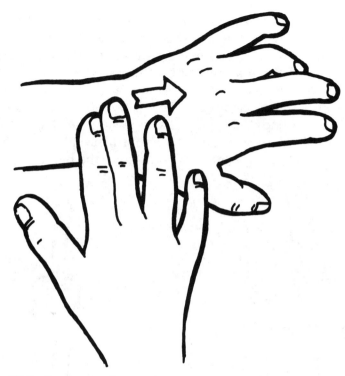

Fig. 29-3. *Push your finger along the vein and the vein disappears.*

Fig. 29-4. *Veins carry blood to the heart.*

arteries. They carry blood away from the heart. The arteries become smaller and smaller as they reach into all areas of the body. The blood moves in spurts that are caused by the heart beat. The blood flows through a tiny mesh of tubes called *capillaries* (Fig. 29-5). These tubes are so small, you need a microscope to see them. Your skin is full of capillaries. This is where the blood delivers material to the body cells and picks up waste. The blood flows into the veins, like the one in the top of your hand. It is a steady flow, and you won't feel a pulse. The veins carry the blood back to the heart.

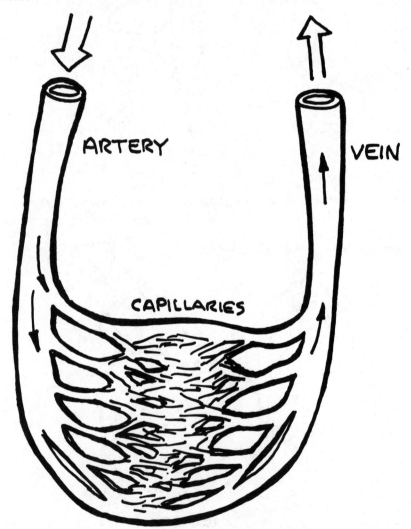

Fig. 29-5. *Arteries carry blood from the heart to the tiny capillaries in the skin.*

30
Listening to Your Heart

Materials
- 2 PLASTIC FUNNELS
- PIECE OF RUBBER TUBING
- WATCH WITH A SECOND HAND
- PENCIL AND PAPER

Connect the rubber tubing to the small ends of the funnels to form a simple stethoscope (Fig. 30-1). Place one funnel over your heart and the other over one ear (Fig. 30-2). Count the number of beats in one minute. Write this number down. Exercise for several seconds (Fig. 30-3), and count the number of beats in one minute. Compare the numbers. Your heart rate should have increased some. It must beat faster because you used up more energy. This forces the blood to remove more waste from your body.

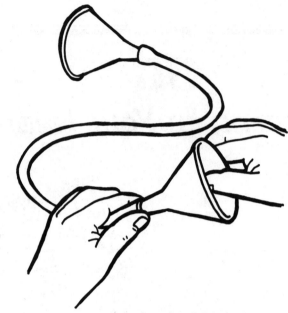

Fig. 30-1. *Insert funnels in each end of the rubber tubing.*

Fig. 30-2. *Count the number of heart beats in one minute.*

Fig. 30-3. *Our heart must beat faster when we use up more energy.*

31
How We See

Ask someone to hold the pencil so that it is pointing straight up, about 2 feet in front of your eyes (Fig. 31-1). Hold one arm straight out from your side with your finger pointing out (Fig. 31-2). Close one eye and slowly bring your arm around and try to place the tip of your finger on the top of the pencil (Fig. 31-3). You will probably miss. Try it a couple of times and then try it with both eyes open. It will be easier. With only one eye, you don't have normal depth perception. Stereoscopic vision is the reason we can judge depths.

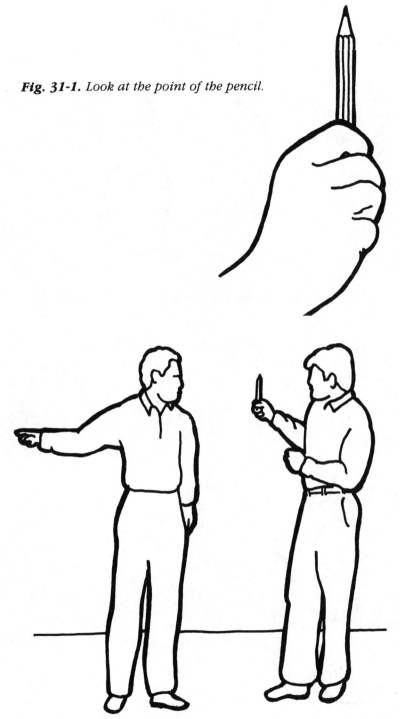

Fig. 31-1. *Look at the point of the pencil.*

Fig. 31-2. *Point your finger out to the side.*

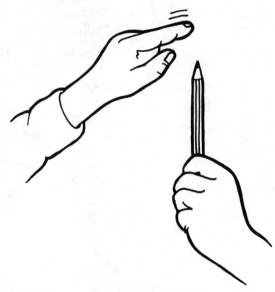

Fig. 31-3. *Close one eye and place the tip of your finger on top of the pencil.*

The brain forms one image from two eyes (Fig. 31-4). The slight differences between the image from the left eye and the image from the right eye allows the brain to determine the distance to the object.

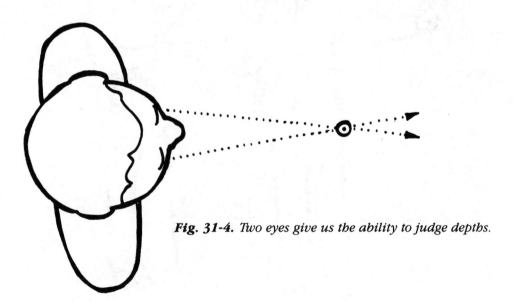

Fig. 31-4. *Two eyes give us the ability to judge depths.*

32
Right-Eyed or Left-Eyed

Materials

PENCIL

DISTANT OBJECT

Hold the pencil straight up in front of you at eye level. Line up the top of the pencil with some object in the distance (Fig. 32-1). Close one eye at a time. You will notice the object moves to one side and then is lined up again. The eye that is open while the object is in line is the dominant eye. Just as people are right-handed or left-handed, they are also right-eyed or left-eyed.

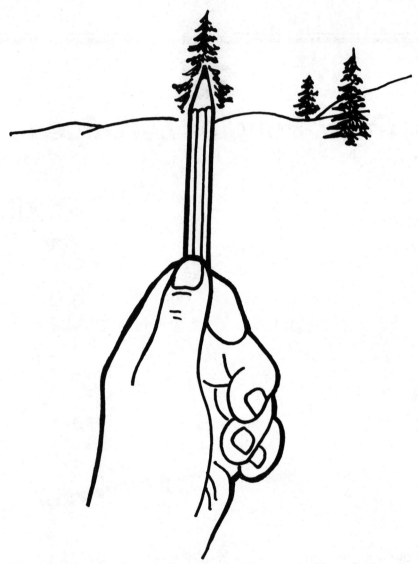

Fig. 32-1. *Line up the pencil with some object in the distance then close one eye.*

33
How We Hear

Materials

- A FRIEND
- CHAIR
- CARDBOARD TUBE FROM PAPER TOWELS
- 2 SPOONS

Ask someone to sit in the chair while you stand behind them. Tell them to point in the direction they hear the sound coming from. Tap the spoons together once about a foot directly behind their head (Fig. 33-1). Then tap the spoons together slightly to one side, then the other. Each time they will be able to point in the correct direction. Ask them to hold one end of the tube against their ear with the other end sticking straight out to the side (Fig. 33-2). Repeat the steps, and this time when you tap the spoons behind the tube, they will think the sound is coming from straight behind their

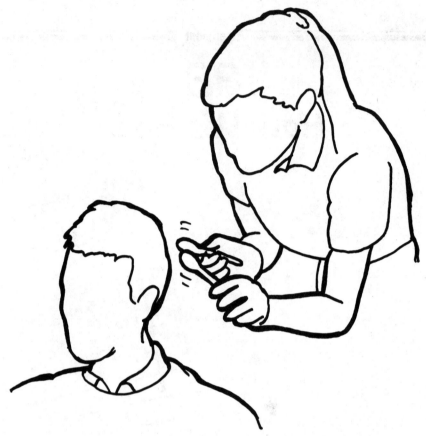

Fig. 33-1. *Tap the spoons together behind someone's head.*

head. This is because our brain can measure the difference between the time it takes sound to reach one ear and the other. When the tube was used, the brain sensed the difference it took for the sound to reach the end of the tube and the other ear.

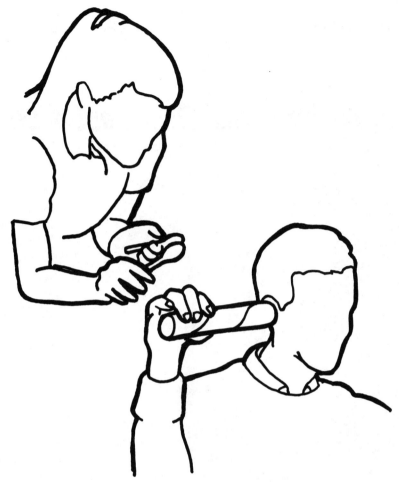

Fig. 33-2. *The cardboard tube confuses their sense of hearing.*

34
Where to Find Our Taste Buds

Materials

TOOTHPICKS
SALTY WATER
SUGAR WATER
LEMON JUICE

Study the illustration (Fig. 34-1), and dip the end of a toothpick into one of the fluids (Fig. 34-2). Touch it to different parts of your tongue (Fig. 34-3), and try to locate the four areas of taste buds; sweet, sour, salty, and bitter. Use a fresh toothpick and try a different sample. Taste happens when the substance is dissolved in a liquid around the taste buds (Fig. 34-4). You cannot taste a piece of dry salt or sugar until some of it has dissolved. The front part of the tongue, the tip and front edges, is sensitive to sweet and salty tastes. The sides are more sensitive to sour, and the back is sensitive to bitter tastes. The center of the tongue is not as sensitive as the edges.

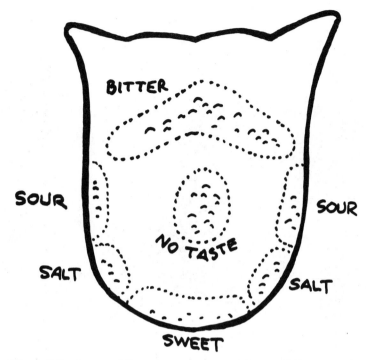

Fig. 34-1. *Areas of the tongue are sensitive to different taste.*

Fig. 34-2. *Use a toothpick to sample one of the fluids.*

Fig. 34-3. *Touch the toothpick to different parts of your tongue.*

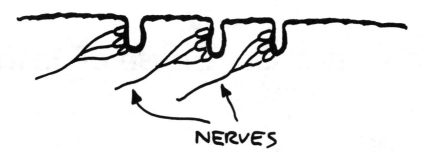

TASTE BUDS

NERVES

Fig. 34-4. *You taste something when it is dissolved around the taste buds.*

35
Odors and Our Sense of Taste

Materials

A SMALL AMOUNT OF DRY, INSTANT COFFEE

Hold your nose, and place a few grains of instant coffee on your tongue (Fig. 35-1). It will quickly start to dissolve but you will not be able to taste it. Continue holding your nose for a few seconds. There still should be no taste, but soon it will be strong. You will probably want to spit out the grains first, then release your nose and inhale. You should quickly taste the coffee. This is why when you have a cold, food seems tasteless. Nerves from the taste buds

Fig. 35-1. *Breathe through your mouth when you place the coffee on your tongue.*

carry signals to the taste center in the brain (Fig. 35-2). The taste center is close to the olfactory (smell) center. The sense of taste and smell are closely related. It is often difficult to tell the difference between the two.

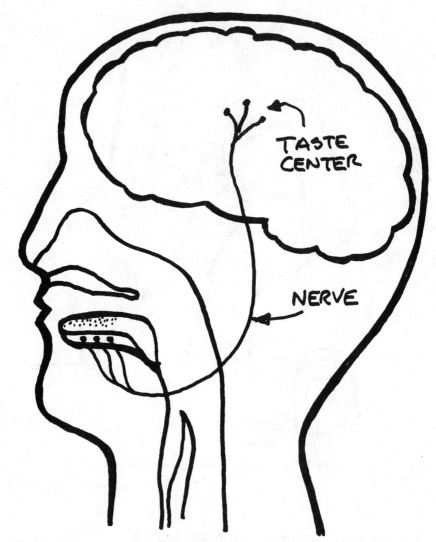

Fig. 35-2. *Nerves from the taste buds carry signals to the brain.*

36
Nerve Endings and
Our Sense of Touch

Materials

A FRIEND
2 PENCILS
TABLE OR DESK

Ask someone to place their arm across a table with the palm up and close their eyes. Hold the pencils next to each other, and touch the person's finger (Fig. 36-1). Ask them to guess how far apart the pencils are. Try it again, except with the pencils separated a couple of inches (Fig. 36-2). The person should be able to guess very close to the actual distance. Try the same experiment on the top of the upper arm (Fig. 36-3). The guess this time should be way off. This is because the nerve endings in our fingers are close together, but they are farther apart in other parts of our body.

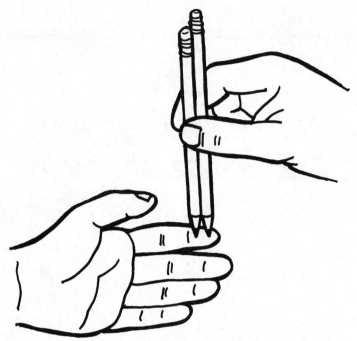

Fig. 36-1. *Hold the pencils together and touch the person's finger.*

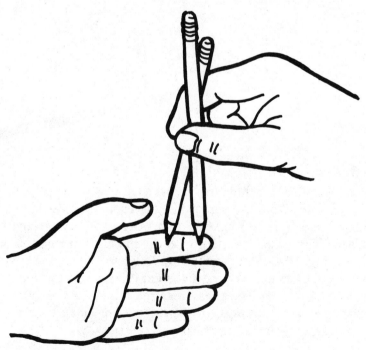

Fig. 36-2. *Touch the finger with the pencils separated.*

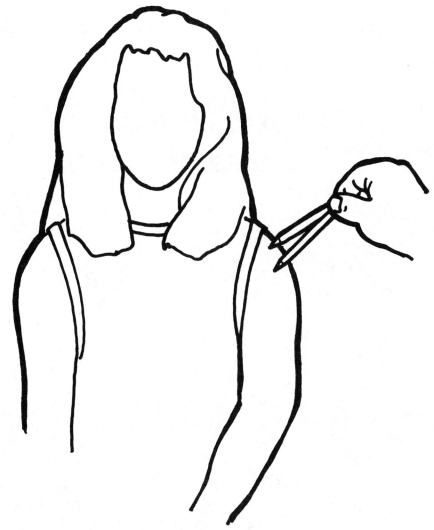

Fig. 36-3. *Nerve endings are farther apart in other areas of our body.*

37

Temperature and Our Sense of Touch

Materials

3 LARGE BOWLS

WATER

Place the bowls in a row on a table, and fill the first one with very cold water. The second with water at room temperature, and the third with very warm water (Fig. 37-1). The water should be hot, but not hot enough to burn you. Place your left hand in the cold water and your right hand in the very warm (Fig. 37-2). Leave them in the water a few seconds. Remove your right hand from the warm water and quickly place it in the center bowl, with the water at room temperature (Fig. 37-3). The water should feel much cooler than it really is. Remove your right hand, and place your left hand from the cold water to the center bowl (Fig. 37-4). The water now

Fig. 37-1. *Place the bowls of water in a row.*

Fig. 37-2. *Place one hand in the cold water and the other hand in the hot water.*

Fig. 37-3. *Remove the hand from the hot water and place it in the water at room temperature.*

Fig. 37-4. *Remove your hand from the cold water and place it in the water at room temperature.*

feels much warmer than it really is. Next, put your left hand back in the cold water and your right hand back in the warm water. Leave them in the water for several seconds. Quickly swap hands. Put the right hand in the cold water and the left hand in the warm water. Notice the differences in the water. In each case, the temperatures you feel should be much greater than the actual temperature of the water. This means that our sense of touch cannot be relied on to determine temperature.

38
Our Sense of Balance

Spread your arms out and try to stand on one foot. Use your arms and the other leg to keep your balance (Fig. 38-1). You will find that looking straight ahead and concentrating on a point will help. With a little practice, you should be able to stay balanced for some time. Try it with your eyes closed. It should be very difficult, even for a few seconds.

Our eyes are very sensitive to movement, and without them, we have to depend on three fluid-filled semicircular canals in our inner ear (Fig. 38-2). When we tilt our head, fluid moves much like water moves when you tilt a glass (Fig. 38-3). This causes changes in

Fig. 38-1. *Try to balance on one foot.*

SEMICIRCULAR CANALS

Fig. 38-2. *There are three fluid-filled canals in our inner ear.*

Fig. 38-3. *The fluid in the canals moves when we tilt our head.*

pressure in the canals. Nerves here send impulses to the brain (Fig. 38-4). The brain interprets the impulses as changes in the position of the body, and sends messages to the muscles that we use to maintain our balance. But, it is difficult to stay balanced with our eyes closed because our eyes are quicker at detecting motion.

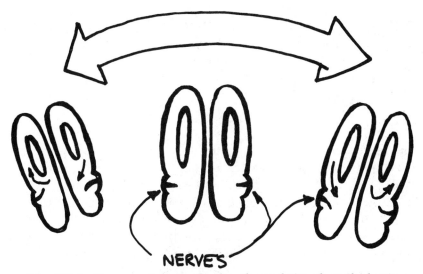

NERVES

Fig. 38-4. *Nerve endings in the canals send signals to the brain.*

39
Why We Get Dizzy

Materials

REVOLVING STOOL

Sit on the stool and spin yourself in one direction (Fig. 39-1). Continue spinning for several seconds and then stop abruptly. It will seem as if the surroundings are whirling around. This is because the fluid in the semicircular canals in the ear continues to move (Fig. 39-2). This sends signals to the brain, and it thinks you are still spinning, but you're not. The brain has problems directing the muscles that keep you balanced. Soon, the fluid in the canals settles down, and you are no longer dizzy.

Fig. 39-1. *Spin in one direction for several seconds.*

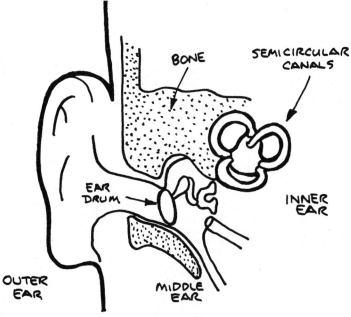

Fig. 39-2. *After you stop spinning, the fluid in the canals in the ear continue to move.*

Science Fairs

Science fairs are a fun part of learning. Building a science fair project can be an exciting experience, but it will require some planning—not enough to be discouraging. A little organization and planning is important if the project is to be successful. Probably the most important part of the planning is deciding on the subject. This requires some research and a lot of thought. If a subject is selected without enough thought, you might find later that you couldn't get the materials or they may have been too expensive, or the project might turn out to be just too complicated to complete. If this occurs, the project is often abandoned and it is usually too late to start another one.

To make the planning easier, you may want to divide your project into a series of easy steps. This will give you a feeling of accomplishment as you complete each step, and you will always be aware of the progress you're making. The steps could be (1) choosing a subject; (2) forming questions and the hypothesis, your guess of what the results of your experiment will be; (3) doing the experiment; and (4) recording the results of your experiment and the conclusions that you formed based on those results.

A research paper can be an important part of your planning (Fig. 40-1). It will help you gather crucial information and will allow you to narrow your subject down to a specific topic. You also might consider making a report on your experiment. This can show what you wanted to prove or a question you wanted to answer. Graphs and charts might be helpful in explaining your project (Fig. 40-2). Your report should include a description of your experiment, the results of your experiment, and the conclusions that you made from conducting the experiment.

When selecting a project, choose something you are really interested in, or a subject that you would like to know more about. Pick a subject that you are enthusiastic about, but not one that is too complicated. Very complicated experiments can sometimes

Fig. 40-1. *A research paper is very helpful when planning a science fair project.*

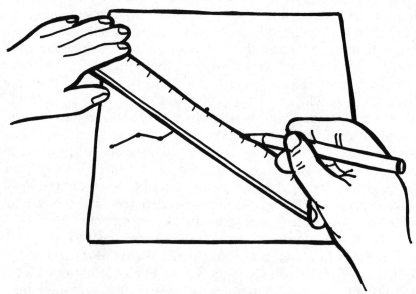

Fig. 40-2. *Grafts and charts can be useful in explaining your project.*

turn into an experience that is filled with frustrations and disappointment. A simple experiment, well demonstrated, can be much more successful than a complicated one that is poorly performed. Some of the greatest scientific breakthroughs were discovered using simple equipment.

Materials for your project don't have to be exotic. Often, you can use items that are commonly found in the trash such as coffee cans, plastic or glass bottles, cardboard tubes from paper towels, and wooden spools from sewing thread (Fig. 40-3). Models for items in your experiment can usually be made from wood or cardboard. Just be creative and use your imagination.

Fig. 40-3. *Throwaway items can often be used to build a science fair project.*

After you have selected a topic for your project, narrow it down to a specific point to prove or a question to be answered. You don't want to generalize. For example, the human body would be too general a subject. Narrow it down to something like what are fingernails made of and why do we have them (Fig. 40-4). Have a definite problem to solve. If you wanted to explore lower forms

Fig. 40-4. *Even fingernails could be the subject of a science fair project.*

of life, you might narrow it down to the kind that is beneficial to humans (Fig. 40-5). You could single out a particular insect, explain its life cycle, and show ways the use of this insect can be expanded to benefit everyone.

If you were interested in how we breathe, you could build a movable model of the lungs, explain what they do and detail the health hazards of polluted air (Fig. 40-6). Something about birds could be narrowed down to one species that might be endangered, why it should be protected, and what could be done to make sure it survived (Fig. 40-7).

Your experiment will probably be displayed on a table or some type of platform. It could be set up in front of a cardboard or wooden panel. The panel could be divided into three sections. The two end sections may be angled forward so that the panel

Fig. 40-5. *The earthworm is surprisingly beneficial to humans.*

Fig. 40-6. *A model of the lungs could show how we breathe and the effects of pollution.*

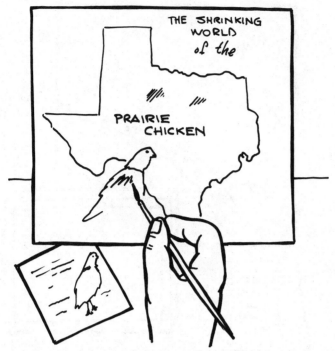

Fig. 40-7. *Some birds are on the endangered list.*

stands by itself. Each section of the panel can display the information from your report. The left section could show the purpose of your experiment. This could include why you selected the project and what you wanted to prove. The middle section of the panel could cover details of how your experiment was constructed, and why it was built the way it was. The right section of the panel could explain the results of your experiment, and the conclusions you made. It also might include any possible uses, or applications for the information gained from your experiment (Fig. 40-8).

By using your imagination, almost any simple experiment can be expanded and developed into a very interesting and educational project. One that you will be proud to share with your family and friends.

Biology is the fascinating science that studies the living things that are all-round us. And many opportunities are just waiting to be discovered and explored by inquiring minds.

Fig. 40-8. *Information can be displayed on panels behind your science fair project.*

Glossary

algae Simple plants with no true stem, root, or leaf.

arteries Tubelike blood vessels that carry blood from the heart to other parts of the body.

biosphere The zone of the earth, extending from its crust out into the surrounding atmosphere that supports life.

blood veins Vessels conveying blood back to the heart from the various organs of the body.

capillaries Tiny tubes that carry blood from the arteries to the veins.

carbon dioxide A colorless, odorless, nonflammable gas, somewhat heavier than air, that passes out of the lungs in breathing.

chrysalis The pupa of some insects.

cocoon A special envelope constructed by the larva for protection during the pupal stage.

compound A material made up of two or more elements joined together.

diaphragm The partition of muscles and tendons between the chest cavity and the abdominal cavity; the midriff.

element A material made up of only one kind of atom.

hibernation The act of spending the winter in a dormant state.

humus A brown or black substance resulting from the partial decay of plant and animal matter; organic part of the soil.

hypothesis A guess used by scientists to explain how or why something happens.

inner ear A section of the ear that contains the balancing organ.

larvae The early immature form of animals that changes structurally when it becomes an adult.

membranes A thin, soft, pliable sheet or layer, especially of animal or vegetable tissue, serving as a covering or lining.

nerve endings The free end of a nerve or nerve fiber.

nitrogen   A colorless, tasteless, odorless gaseous chemical element.

olfactory   Pertaining to the sense of smell.

pupa   Any insect in the nonfeeding stage of development between the last larval and adult form.

saturated   Having absorbed all that can be taken up.

stereoscopic vision   The ability to have depth perception. Each eye sees a slightly different view of the same object. Your brain coordinates the two views to form a three-dimensional image.

stethoscope   A tube adapted for listening to the sounds produced in the body.

taste buds   Any of the cells that are embedded in the tongue and functioning as the sense organs of taste.

Index

Other Bestsellers of Related Interest

BOTANY: 49 Science Fair Projects
—Robert L. Bonnet and G. Daniel Keen

A rich source of project ideas for teachers, parents and youth leaders, *Botany* introduces children ages 8 through 13 to the wonder and complexity of the natural world through worthwhile, and often environmentally timely, experimentation. Projects are grouped categorically under plant germination, photosynthesis, hydroponics, plant tropism, plant cells, seedless plants, and plant dispersal. Each experiment contains a subject overview, materials list, problem identification, hypothesis, procedures and further research suggestions. Numerous illustrations and tables are included. 176 pages, 149 illustrations. Book No. 3277, $9.95 paperback $16.95 hardcover

EARTH SCIENCE: 49 Science Fair Projects
—Robert L. Bonnet and G. Daniel Keen

This is an excellent resource for cultivating a better understanding of planet Earth among children ages 8-13. By studying the forces at work around them, they develop an appreciation for the foundations of science—concise thinking, clear notes and data gathering, curiosity and patience—which can carry over to every aspect of their lives. Projects include: growing crystals, solar distillery, erosion, weather forecasting, and more. 160 pages, 43 illustrations. Book No. 3287, $9.95 paperback $16.95 hardcover

PHYSICS FOR KIDS: 49 Easy Experiments with Electricity and Magnetism
—Robert W. Wood

What makes a magnet stick to the refrigerator? What makes the batteries in a flashlight work? Find the answers to these questions, and more, in this entertaining and instructional project book. These quick, safe, and inexpensive experiments include making items like: a magnet, potato battery, flashlight, compass, telegraph, model railroad signal, and electric lock. 142 pages, 151 illustrations. Book No. 3412, $9.95 paperback $16.95 hardcover

PHYSICS FOR KIDS: 49 Easy Experiments with Heat—Robert W. Wood

This volume introduces thermodynamics, or the physics of heat, to students ages 8-13. By performing these safe, simple experiments, kids can begin to understand the principles of conduction, convection, and radiation. Experiments show students how to: make a thermometer, make invisible ink, measure body heat, pull a wire through an ice cube, all quick, safe, and inexpensive, with results in less than 30 minutes. 160 pages, 162 illustrations. Book No. 3292, $9.95 paperback $16.95 hardcover

PHYSICS FOR KIDS: 49 Easy Experiments with Optics—Robert W. Wood

Young readers ages 8-13 will enjoy these quick and easy experiments that provide a thorough introduction to what light is, how it behaves, and how it can be put to work. Wood provides projects including: making a kaleidoscope and a periscope, an ice lens, and a pinhole camera; and learning why stars twinkle, and how a mirror works. Projects produce results often in less than 30 minutes and require only common household items to complete. 178 pages, 164 illustrations. Book No. 3402, $9.95 paperback $16.95 hardcover

333 SCIENCE TRICKS AND EXPERIMENTS
—Robert J. Brown
"Well-described and aptly illustrated."
—New Technical Books

Here is a delightful collection of experiments and "tricks" that demonstrate a variety of well-known, and not so well-known, scientific principles and illusions. Find tricks based on inertia, momentum, and sound projects based on biology, water surface tension, gravity and centrifugal force, heat, and light. Every experiment is easy to understand and construct and uses ordinary household items. 208 pages, 189 illustrations. Book No. 1825, $9.95 paperback $16.95 hardcover

THROUGH THE TELESCOPE: A Guide for the Amateur Astronomer—Michael R. Porcellino

Through the Telescope is an open invitation to explore our universe. This book and an amateur astronomical telescope are all you need to meet the multitude of stars, nebulae, and deep-sky objects that can be seen on a dark, clear night. Porcellino guides you on a tour of the Moon, where you'll visit craters, mountains and rilles, and learn to identify their unique features. Next you'll move out to the satellites of Jupiter, the rings of Saturn, and the Sun. 352 pages, 217 illustrations. Book No. 3159, $18.95 paperback $26.95 hardcover

HOMEMADE HOLOGRAMS: The Complete Guide to Inexpensive, Do-It-Yourself Holography—John Iovine

Make your own holograms, easily and inexpensively with this breakthrough book. John Iovine tells you how to produce laser-generated images plus equipment like a portable isolation table and a helium-neon laser. You'll also construct devices that can make your experiments easier and more professional, such as magnetic film holders, spatial filters, an electronic shutter, an audible electronic timer, and a laser power meter and photometer. 240 pages, 185 illustrations. Book No. 3460, $14.95 paperback $22.95 hardcover